STUDY GUIDE

God Alone

R.C. Sproul

LIGONIER MINISTRIES
Renew your Mind.
LIGONIER.ORG | 800-435-4343

421 Ligonier Court, Sanford, FL 32771
E-mail: info@ligonier.org

Printed in the United States of America.

1

Sola Fide

MESSAGE INTRODUCTION

The argument that justification is sola fide, or by faith alone, was a central issue in the sixteenth-century Protestant Reformation. The Roman Catholic Church asserted that justification is by faith with the addition of works. The Reformers argued that man's justification is by faith alone with the addition of no works or merit by man. The growth of subjective doctrine and relativism reveals the importance of defining a true doctrine of man's justification today. In this lecture, Dr. Sproul discusses sola fide.

SCRIPTURE READING

Genesis 12

LEARNING OBJECTIVES

1. To identify the five solas of the Protestant Reformation.
2. To emphasize the significance of the debate over justification in the sixteenth century.
3. To define the Roman Catholic doctrine of justification.

QUOTATION

"When Abraham shall rise again, at the last day, then he will chide us for our unbelief, and will say: I had not the hundredth part of the promises which ye have, and yet I believed. That example of Abraham exceeds all human natural reason, who, overcoming the paternal love he bore towards his only son Isaac, was all obedient to God, and, against the law of nature, would have sacrificed that son. What, for the space of three days, he felt in his breast, how his heart yearned and panted, what hesitations and trials he had, cannot be expressed."

—Martin Luther

LECTURE OUTLINE

A. The five solas were rallying points of the Protestant Reformation.
   1. Sola Fide = Faith Alone
   2. Sola Gratia = Grace Alone
   3. Solus Christus = Christ Alone
   4. Sola Scriptura = Scripture Alone
   5. Soli Deo Gloria = Glory to God Alone

B. The Protestant assertion that salvation is sola fide or through faith alone was a central issue in the sixteenth century Protestant Reformation.
   - The Protestant Reformers argued that man's justification is by faith alone with the addition of no works or merit by man.

C. The debate over man's justification before God was a significant issue in the sixteenth century.
   - The question of man's justification receives less attention today because of the dominance of relativism.

D. The biblical truth of man's condemnation outside of God's justification needs to be preached and taught in the modern church.
   - Many in the church do not truly believe in the doctrine of justification by faith alone and therefore do not emphasize it.

E. The Gospel's emphasis on the deliverance of man from God's wrath has been forgotten in many Christian circles.
   1. The Gospel does not simply deliver us from bad habits, addictions, social failure, psychological deficiency, and broken relationships.
   2. The central focus of the Gospel is delivering sinners from the judgment of God.

F. The Roman Catholic Church historically has argued that justification is through faith, grace, and Christ, but not through these avenues alone.
   1. The Roman Catholic Church teaches that faith is the initiation, foundation, and root of justification.
   2. The Church teaches that grace is necessary for justification.
   3. The Church also affirms the atonement of Christ as necessary for man's justification.

G. The Roman Catholic Church does not believe that justification is by faith alone, grace alone, or Christ alone.
   1. The Roman Church teaches that justification is through faith plus our works, grace plus our merit, and Christ plus ourselves that brings us justification.
   2. The Reformers rejected the idea that man can perform good works, produce merit, or exhibit the personal righteousness necessary for salvation.

H. The Roman Catholic Church views baptism as the "instrumental cause" or method of justification.
   1. The Church believes that upon baptism people receive an infusion of grace.

  2. A baptized member of the church is justified if he assents to the infusion of grace and he does not commit a mortal sin.
  3. The sacrament of penance brings forgiveness in the event of a mortal sin.
  4. Justification is acquired in the Roman Catholic Church through the instruments of the sacraments.

I. The Reformers argued that the instrumental cause of justification is not through any sacrament or work, but rather through faith in Christ alone.

STUDY QUESTIONS

1. The Protestant assertion that salvation is __________ or through faith alone was a central issue in the Protestant Reformation.
   a. Sola Fide
   b. Sola Gratia
   c. Solus Christus
   d. Sola Scriptura

2. The debate over man's justification before God was a significant issue in the __________ century.
   a. fourteenth
   b. fifteenth
   c. sixteenth
   d. seventeenth

3. The question of man's justification receives less attention today because of the dominance of __________.
   a. relativism
   b. Orthodoxy
   c. Catholicism
   d. Protestantism

4. The Roman Catholic Church teaches that __________ is the initiation, foundation, and root of justification.
   a. grace
   b. faith
   c. baptism
   d. penance

5. The Roman Catholic Church views __________ as the "instrumental cause" or method of justification.
   a. penance
   b. baptism
   c. the Lord's Supper
   d. extreme unction

6. The __________ rejected the idea that man can perform good works, produce merit, or exhibit the personal righteousness necessary for salvation.
   a. Roman Catholics
   b. Orthodox Christians
   c. Reformers
   d. humanists

7. The Church believes that upon baptism people receive an infusion of __________.
   a. grace
   b. works
   c. perfection
   d. prayer

8. The Reformers argued that the instrumental cause of justification is not through any sacrament or work, but rather through __________.
   a. faith alone
   b. baptism
   c. the last rites
   d. the Church

BIBLE STUDY

1. What is the command God gives Abram at the beginning of Genesis 12? Why would this be a particularly challenging command for Abram's time and culture?

2. What role will God play in blessing Abram? What is Abram's role?

3. What is Abram's reaction to God's command? Do you think Abram's actions were difficult?

4. What does Abram do every time he moves to a new location? What do you believe is the significance of this practice?

5. What was Abram's fear as he and his wife entered Egypt? How does he take his circumstances into his own hands and fail to trust God?

6. What are the two sides of Abram's character revealed in this chapter? How can you relate or not relate to Abram?

DISCUSSION QUESTIONS

1. What significant test of faith has God allowed you to experience? What was your reaction to this experience?

2. How is God currently calling you to faith and obedience even though the road ahead is obscured? What does your faith look like amidst what seems to be senseless suffering and disappointment?

3. Do you have the faith to believe that where you are today is exactly where God wants you? How does the life of Abraham discourage you away from manipulation and encourage you towards a life of trust?

4. What role does faith play in listening to the voice of God? How does what we believe about God affect how we listen to Him?

5. What are the truths you know in your head, but yet are very difficult to believe in your heart?

APPLICATION

1. Ask the Lord to give you the faith you need to follow Him in obedience regardless of your current circumstances.

2. Consider how you are tempted to replace your faith with the thinking of this world.

FOR FURTHER STUDY

Sproul, R.C. *Faith Alone*
Kistler, Don, ed. *Justification by Faith Alone*
Buchanan, James *The Doctrine of Justification*

2

Sola Fide

MESSAGE INTRODUCTION

The justification of sinners was the central issue of debate for Martin Luther during the Protestant Reformation. The Roman Catholic Church asserted that man was justified by faith with the addition of meritorious works. Luther argued from Scripture that justification is from beginning to end the work of God. It is only through faith that man can embrace the grace of God with no credit to himself. In this lecture, Dr. Sproul continues to discuss the doctrine of justification by faith alone.

SCRIPTURE READING

Genesis 15–17

LEARNING OBJECTIVES

1. To outline the Roman Catholic doctrine of justification.
2. To discuss the Protestant response to the Roman Catholic doctrine of justification.
3. To discuss the impact of the events of the sixteenth century on the debate over justification.

QUOTATION

"Faith's substance is our will; its manner is, that we take hold on Christ by divine instinct; its final cause and fruit, that it purifies the heart, makes us children of God, and brings with it the remission of sins."

—Martin Luther

LECTURE OUTLINE

A. The Protestant Reformation was in large part a controversy over how a man or woman is justified by God.
   1. The Roman Catholic Church argued that man is not justified by faith alone and apart from other works.
   2. The Protestant Reformers argued that man is justified by faith alone apart from any other works.

B. The Pope argued that he had the authority to free people from purgatory through the sale of indulgences.

C. The church called the sacrament of penance the second plank of justification for those who lost their justification by committing a mortal sin.
   1. The sacrament of penance required the confession of sin, a prayer of contrition, and priestly absolution.
   2. Works of satisfaction were the final component of the sacrament of penance, which were to satisfy the demands of God's Law.
   3. Works of satisfaction earned the penitent merit with God.

D. "Condign" merit reflects the worthiness of the penitent and "congruous" merit reflects the works of the penitent.

E. The giving of alms was one work of satisfaction defined by the Roman Catholic Church.
   - Giving to the poor could earn the penitent his works of satisfaction.

F. The Papacy emphasized the importance of a repentant heart, but indulgence hawkers such as Johann Tetzel seemed to send the message that one could buy his salvation.

G. Martin Luther attacked the abuses of the Church's sacrament of penance and then eventually attacked the doctrine itself.

H. The Church held the power of the keys to transfer a portion of the treasury of merit to those in purgatory who lacked sufficient merit.
   1. The treasury of merit included the merits of Christ, the holy family, and all the saints.
   2. A penitent individual is justified if they share in the treasury of merit.
   3. A person is justified unless they commit mortal sin in which case if they die they descend directly to hell.

I. The sacrament of extreme unction is a safeguard against the individual dying with mortal sin.
   1. According to the Church most people do not die with mortal sin, but venial sin in which case they go to purgatory in order to be purged of any impurities.
   2. Very few people go directly to heaven and most go to purgatory.

J. Saints with plenty of righteous merit go directly to heaven and their remaining merit is deposited in the treasury of merit.

- The Pope had the power to transfer the surplus merit of the saints to those in need of merit in purgatory.

K. Martin Luther said that if the Pope was good he would empty the treasury of merit and free many souls from purgatory.
   - Luther saw this Catholic doctrine as a radical distortion of the merits of Christ and the biblical doctrine of justification.

L. The Roman Catholic Church argued that justification is analytical and based on inherent righteousness.
   - The Catholic Church argued for infused righteousness which is the merits of Christ plus human cooperation.

M. The Protestant doctrine of justification argued for imparted righteousness wherein the merits of Christ are received apart from any works of man.

N. The New Testament doctrine of the atonement means not only that Christ suffered for us, but that He also lived in righteousness for us.
   - It is impossible for man to be justified apart from the perfect character of the Son of God.

O. Faith is the instrument through which man embraces Christ.
   1. A believer is clothed with the righteousness of Christ through faith alone.
   2. The righteousness of Christ is an alien righteousness to the individual because it is foreign to the recipient.

P. Jesus' performance is transferred to the believer with no credit going to the believer.
   - God calls the believer just before He makes him just.

Q. The imputation of the righteousness of Christ to the believer apart from any effort on the part of the believer is at the heart of the Gospel.

STUDY QUESTIONS

1. The Protestant Reformation was in large part a controversy over how a man or woman is __________ by God.
   a. judged
   b. compensated
   c. justified
   d. forgotten

2. The Pope argued he had the authority to free people from purgatory through the sale of __________.
   a. cathedrals
   b. relics
   c. indulgences
   d. icons

3. The church called the sacrament of penance the second plank of justification for those who lost their justification by committing a __________ sin.
   a. venial
   b. mortal
   c. heinous
   d. minor

4. The sacrament of __________ required the confession of sin, a prayer of contrition, and priestly absolution.
   a. the eucharist
   b. penance
   c. extreme unction
   d. ordination

5. __________ merit reflects the worthiness of the penitent.
   a. Condign
   b. Congruous
   c. Controlled
   d. Central

6. __________ was one work of satisfaction defined by the Roman Catholic Church.
   a. Bible study
   b. The giving of alms
   c. Teaching Sunday school
   d. Building cathedrals

7. The Church held the power of the keys to transfer a portion of the treasury of merit to those in __________ who lacked sufficient merit.
   a. heaven
   b. hell
   c. purgatory
   d. the grave

8. __________ is the instrument through which man embraces Christ.
   a. Extreme Unction
   b. Baptism
   c. Faith
   d. Confession

BIBLE STUDY

1. What is the promise God gives to Abram in Gen. 15:1? How does Abram seek to secure a promise he does not believe he will receive? (15:2-3)

2. What is the ceremony Abram witnesses in Gen. 15? How is God seeking to strengthen Abram's faith with this ceremony? How is God currently working to strengthen your faith?

3. How does Sarai take things into her own hands and refuse to trust God in Gen. 16? What are the negative consequences that result from this act of mistrust?

4. Who are the people who are hurt the most by Abram and Sarai's disbelief in God's promises?

5. Why do you think God repeats His promises to Abram and Sarai in Gen. 17:1-8? Why do you think God changed the names of Abram and Sarai to Abraham and Sarah?

6. What is the sign that God requires of Abraham as a symbol of covenant loyalty? What is the sign that God requires of believers today as a symbol of our faithfulness to the New Covenant?

DISCUSSION QUESTIONS

1. God did not meet Abraham's expectations regarding a child until very late in life. In what areas of your life has God not met your expectations? How do you struggle to have faith and trust Him amidst such circumstances?

2. Abraham put more faith in his plan to have a child through Hagar than God's plan for him to have a child through Sarah. How are you tempted to put more of your faith in your ideas about God rather than God Himself?

3. What is the relationship between taking risks with God and waiting for Him to act?

4. In what ways is it difficult for you to wait on God?

APPLICATION

1. Ask God to give you the faith to trust Him despite your current circumstances.

2. Consider how the Lord is currently challenging you to take the words of Jesus, "follow me," seriously.

FOR FURTHER STUDY

Sproul, R.C. *Faith Alone*
Kistler, Don, ed. *Justification by Faith Alone*
Buchanan, James *The Doctrine of Justification*
Fesko, J.V. *Justification*

3

Sola Gratia

MESSAGE INTRODUCTION

The Pelagian controversy was a key conflict in the history of the church near the end of the fourth century. The teachings of Pelagius regarding justification and the fall began to spread so rapidly that Saint Augustine felt compelled to combat them with a doctrine of salvation grounded in Scripture. Along with the endorsement of the Church, Saint Augustine exposed the Pelagian heresy and reasserted an orthodox defense of the doctrine salvation by grace alone. In this lecture, Dr. Sproul discusses the truth that salvation is by grace alone.

SCRIPTURE READING

Exodus 1-15

LEARNING OBJECTIVES

1. To outline the teachings of Pelagius regarding the Fall and justification.
2. To discuss the impact of the Fall on the nature of all men.
3. To describe Augustine's response to the teachings of Pelagius.

QUOTATION

"As grace is first from God, so it is continually from him, as much as light is all day long from the sun, as well as at first dawn or at sun-rising."

—Jonathan Edwards

LECTURE OUTLINE

A. Sola Gratiae or "grace alone" was also a significant doctrine during the Protestant Reformation.
B. St. Augustine is known as the doctor gratiae or the "doctor of grace" because of his emphasis on the grace of God in salvation.
C. *"Justification by faith alone is a truth that needs interpretation. The principle of sola fide is not rightly understood until it is seen as anchored in the broader principle of sola gratiae. What is the source and status of faith? Is it the God given means whereby the God given justification is received or is it a condition of justification which is left to man for fulfillment? Is it a part of God's gift of salvation or man's own contribution to salvation? Is our salvation wholly of God or does it ultimately depend on something we do for ourselves? Those who say the latter thereby deny man's utter helplessness in sin and affirm that a form of semi-Pelagianism is true after all. It is no wonder then that later Reformed theology condemned Arminianism as being in principle a return to Rome because in effect it turned faith into a meritorious work and was a betrayal of the Reformation because it denied the sovereignty of God in saving sinners which was the deepest religious and theological principle of the Reformer's thought. Arminianism was in Reformed eyes a renunciation of New Testament Christianity in favor of New Testament Judaism. For to rely on oneself for faith is no different in principle than relying on oneself for works and the one is as unchristian and as anti-Christian as the other. In the light of what Luther says to Erasmus there is no doubt that he would have endorsed this judgment."* (Johnson/Packer)
D. Arminians affirm justification by faith alone and that no man can be saved by his works.
E. Adhering to unchristian ideas or thoughts does not mean necessarily that a person is not a Christian.
F. The doctrine of original sin and the doctrine of election are closely related to the concept of sola gratiae.
G. The Pelagian controversy occurred near the end of the fourth century.
    1. The British monk Pelagius visited Rome and was appalled by the immorality of the clergy in Rome.
    2. Pelagius was disturbed by Augustine's prayer: *"O God, grant what thou dost command and command what thou dost desire."*
H. Man was created with a mandate to be holy, righteous, and perfect.
    - The Fall so corrupted man's nature that it is impossible for him to do any good or choose God apart from the gracious intervention of God.
I. Pelagius argued that the sin of Adam only affected Adam and there was no transfer of a sin nature to his offspring.
    1. Man not only sins from a sin nature, but rather when he imitates Adam's behavior.
    2. Adam did not change man's essential nature.
    3. Man is born today with the very same nature Adam had when he was originally created.

4. Pelagius argued that some people do choose to live righteous lives.
5. The moral ability to achieve perfection remains within man even after the fall.
6. Grace facilitates the ability to live a righteous life, but is not necessary for a person to be righteous.

J. The Roman Catholic Church condemned the theology of Pelagius as heretical in the fifth and sixteenth centuries.

K. Augustine argued that the Fall was so disabling that man was placed into a condition of spiritual death and moral inability to do the things of God.

L. Some people demonstrate a "civic righteousness" or outward righteousness to do good, but no one has a natural inclination for the things of God.
   1. The heart of a fallen individual is a heart of stone.
   2. Man is powerless to do good apart from the intervention of God.

STUDY QUESTIONS

1. ___________ is known as the "doctor of grace" due to his emphasis on God's grace in his doctrine of justification.
   a. St. Augustine
   b. Martin Luther
   c. Pelagius
   d. Thomas Aquinas

2. The doctrine of original sin and the doctrine of election are closely related to the concept of ___________.
   a. sola gratiae.
   b. sola fide
   c. solus Christus
   d. sola scriptura

3. The Pelagian controversy occurred near the end of the ___________ century.
   a. third
   b. fourth
   c. fifth
   d. sixth

4. The British monk ___________ visited Rome and was appalled by the immorality of the clergy in Rome.
   a. Augustine
   b. Pelagius
   c. Aquinas
   d. Calvin

5. __________ argued that the sin of Adam only affected Adam and there was no transfer of a sin nature to his offspring.
   a. Augustine
   b. Pelagius
   c. Aquinas
   d. Calvin

6. The Roman Catholic Church condemned the theology of __________ as heretical in the fifth and sixteenth centuries.
   a. Augustine
   b. Pelagius
   c. Aquinas
   d. Calvin

7. __________ argued that the Fall was so disabling that man was placed into a condition of spiritual death and moral inability to do the things of God.
   a. Augustine
   b. Pelagius
   c. Aquinas
   d. Calvin

8. Civic Righteousness is an outward display of righteousness lacking: __________
   a. perfect holiness
   b. inner transformation
   c. an alien righteousness
   d. all of the above

BIBLE STUDY

1. How can you see the irresistible call of God's grace operating in the life of Moses? How does God work in his life to draw Moses unto Himself? How has God done the same in your life?

2. How is God the prime mover in bringing about the deliverance of the Israelites? (Ex. 2:23-25) How is God the prime mover in the salvation of a soul?

3. How does God's call to Moses parallel the call of God on a dead heart?

4. What is the reaction of Pharaoh's heart to Moses' plea to free the Israelites? Who is responsible for Pharaoh's hard heart?

5. Read Ex. 6:1. Why does Pharaoh eventually demonstrate an outward obedience to God's will although his inner heart remains unchanged? Why do other unregenerate hearts demonstrate an exterior righteousness apart from an interior regeneration?

6. How does Moses demonstrate a growing measure of faith in God's plan and power in the early chapters of Exodus? What can you learn about sanctification from his example?

DISCUSSION QUESTIONS

1. God not only issues the initial call of grace in the believer's heart, but continues to extend His grace over the lifetime of a believer. How can you see evidence of God's grace throughout the life of Moses? How can you see evidence of His grace throughout your life?

2. How did the call of Moses leave no room for individual pride or boasting? How is the call of God's grace similar?

3. What is the call God has placed on your life that requires you to trust His grace? What do you hope you could accomplish that will require God's intervention from beginning to end?

APPLICATION

1. Consider how the struggle of Moses to believe God's call on his life comforts you in your own faith struggles.

2. Ask the Lord to show you how He is calling you to trust Him and His grace alone during this period of your life.

FOR FURTHER STUDY

Sproul, R.C. *Willing to Believe*
Sproul, R.C. *What is Reformed Theology?*
Luther, Martin *The Bondage of the Will*
Ferguson, Sinclair *By Grace Alone*

4

Sola Gratia

MESSAGE INTRODUCTION

The conflict between the Augustinian and Pelagian view of salvation is one of the most significant debates over salvation in history. The semi-Pelagian view was an attempt to find a middle ground between these two positions. The semi-Pelagians argued that the fall may have impaired man's moral ability to choose God, yet he is still able to demonstrate a righteous choice by choosing the forgiveness of Christ. In contrast, Reformed theology has argued that man cannot choose to receive God's grace unless God first brings regeneration to the human heart. In this lecture, Dr. Sproul discusses the truth that salvation is by grace alone.

SCRIPTURE READING

Romans 3, 9

LEARNING OBJECTIVES

1. To explain the historical background of Semi-Pelagianism.
2. To identify the primary tenets of the Semi-Pelagian doctrine of salvation.
3. To identify the primary tenets of an Augustinian doctrine of salvation.

QUOTATIONS

"Grace is but glory begun, and glory is but grace perfected."

—Jonathan Edwards

"Nor can a man with grace his soul inspire, More than the candles set themselves on fire."

—John Bunyan

LECTURE OUTLINE

A. St. Augustine's emphasis on salvation by grace alone developed out of his conflict with the heretic Pelagius.
   - Pelagianism resurfaced in the sixteenth century Socinian movement and in the nineteenth century movements of liberalism and Finneyism.

B. Semi-Pelagianism is an attempt to find a middle ground between Augustinian thought and Pelagian thought.
   1. Augustinian theology was labeled new and inconsistent with the church fathers.
   2. Augustine's teaching regarding predestination cripples preaching and the faith of others.
   3. Augustine overstated man's moral inability after the Fall although the Fall severely crippled man's moral nature.
   4. Semi-Pelagians argue that salvation is a synergistic work between God and man and God's call of grace is resistible.

C. Luther and Calvin argued that man has the ability to make choices after the Fall, but his will is so twisted that he only chooses evil apart from the gracious intervention of God.
   - The classical Reformed position states that man will always choose rebellion over righteousness unless God quickens the Spirit.

D. The doctrine of election is neglected by Semi-Pelagianism because its teachings place the decision of man before the regenerative work of God.

E. God does not owe saving grace to anyone and He is perfectly just if He gives it to nobody.

F. All whom God regenerates receive God's gift of grace through faith.

G. The faith that accompanies God's grace is effectual and cannot fail to regenerate a soul.

H. One individual is not saved over another because of better decision making regarding the offer of grace.

I. Salvation is monergistic and regeneration is solely a work of God.
   - Sanctification is a synergistic work between the spirit of man and the Spirit of God.

STUDY QUESTIONS

1. St. Augustine's emphasis on salvation by grace alone developed out of his conflict with the heretic __________.
   a. Pelagius
   b. Marcion
   c. Origen
   d. Tetzel

2. __________resurfaced in the sixteenth century Socinian movement and in the nineteenth century movements of liberalism and Finneyism.
   a. Augustinianism
   b. Reformed theology
   c. Pelagianism
   d. Gnosticism

3 Semi-Pelagianism is an attempt to find a middle ground between __________ thought and Pelagian thought.
   a. Gnostic
   b. Roman Catholic
   c. Augustinian
   d. Montanist

4. __________ argued that salvation is a synergistic work between God and man and God's call of grace is resistible.
   a. Augustine
   b. Pelagius
   c. Calvin
   d. Luther

5. __________ argued that salvation is monergistic and regeneration is solely a work of God.
   a. Pelagius
   b. Luther
   c. Finney
   d. Aquinas

6. The doctrine of __________ is neglected by Semi-Pelagianism because its teachings place the decision of man before the regenerative work of God.
   a. sanctification
   b. election
   c. glorification
   d. the Holy Spirit

7. __________ is a synergistic work between the spirit of man and the Spirit of God.
   a. Election
   b. Regeneration
   c. Sanctification
   d. Reprobation

8. __________ argued that man has the ability to make choices after the Fall, but his will is so twisted that he only chooses evil apart from the gracious intervention of God.
   a. Pelagius
   b. Finney
   c. Tetzel
   d. Luther

BIBLE STUDY

1. How does Paul describe the human condition in Romans 3:9-20? Does he leave any room for human goodness or wisdom to pursue God?

2. According to Paul what were the benefits that Jews had as the covenant people of God? Did these benefits lead them to consistent national righteousness? Why or why not?

3. How does Paul define the people of God in Rom. 9:6-9? Is participation in the family of God a result of human effort or divine promise?

4. What is the promise Paul is speaking of when he declares only the children of promise are the children of God? How does this fact place God as the primary agent for regenerating the human heart?

5. Why does Paul refer to the births of Jacob and Esau to build his argument about divine election in Rom. 9:10-16? What is the basis of the gift of God's mercy?

6. How does the example of Pharaoh fit into Paul's discussion of divine election? Why does God create individuals like Pharaoh? What does this teach us about the character of God?

7 What should the attitude of believers be if God is the first and primary agent of regeneration? How does God silence man's objections?

8. How does elevating man's ability to choose God diminish the glorious power of God?

DISCUSSION QUESTIONS

1. Why can believers rejoice despite Paul's gloomy report in Romans 3 regarding the depths of man's depravity?

2. How does a proper knowledge of man's sin lead to a broader understanding of God's grace?

3. How does knowing that the divine call of grace is irresistible encourage you in your relationships with nonbelievers? How does this truth remove the pressure from finding effective evangelism strategies?

APPLICATION

1. Reflect on the truth that God chose you before you chose Him.

2. Read Philippians 1:6. Ask God to show you the work He has begun and will by His grace finish in your life.

FOR FURTHER STUDY

Sproul, R.C. *Willing to Believe*
Sproul, R.C. *What is Reformed Theology?*
Luther, Martin *The Bondage of the Will*
Ferguson, Sinclair *By Grace Alone*

5

Solus Christus

MESSAGE INTRODUCTION

God often employed covenants in Scripture to relate to His people. God first offered Adam the covenant of works wherein life was promised for obedience. Adam violated this covenant, and therefore out of His grace God responded with the covenant of grace. This covenant offers the believer a righteous standing before God through the imputed righteousness of Christ apart from any works. The covenant of grace brings salvation through Christ alone. In this lecture, Dr. Sproul discusses the truth that salvation is by Christ alone.

SCRIPTURE READING

John 5, 8, 14

LEARNING OBJECTIVES

1. To identify and define the Covenant of Works.
2. To identify and define the Covenant of Grace.
3. To distinguish between imparted righteousness and imputed righteousness.

QUOTATION

"Christ had neither money, nor riches, nor earthly kingdom, for he gave the same to kings and princes. But he reserved one thing peculiarly to himself, which no human creature or angel could do – namely, to conquer sin and death, the devil and hell, and in the midst of death to deliver and save those that through his word believe in him."

—Martin Luther

LECTURE OUTLINE

A. The Protestant Reformers argued that salvation is by grace alone, through faith alone, because of Christ alone.

B. The basic structure of the relationship between God and His people is found in the covenants of the Bible.

C. The Covenant of Works is distinguished from the Covenant of Grace.

D. *"The distance between God and the creature is so great, that although reasonable creatures do owe obedience unto him as their Creator, yet they could never have any fruition of him as their blessedness and reward, but by some voluntary condescension on God's part, which he hath been pleased to express by way of covenant."* (WCF VII:1)

   1. The creature is naturally in debt to the Creator and that which is made owes obedience to its maker.
   2. God owes us nothing and we owe Him our very lives.
   3. God has by His grace condescended to the lives of His creatures to form a relationship with them.
   4. Every covenant God offers to man is an act of grace.

E. *"The first covenant made with man was a covenant of works, wherein life was promised to Adam, and in him to his posterity, upon condition of perfect and personal obedience." (WCF VII:2)*

   1. Adam and Eve were under a period of probation in the Garden wherein if they obeyed God they would have life and if they disobeyed God they would die.
   2. The Covenant stipulated life or death based on the works of obedience or disobedience of Adam and Eve.
   3. The disobedience of one man brought death upon the entire human race.

F. Believers in Christ are not only restored to the innocence Adam held before the Fall, but also participate in all the glories and benefits of Christ.

   - The eternal inheritance of believers in Christ is greater than Adam's state before the Fall.

G. *"Man by his fall having made himself incapable of life by that covenant, the Lord was pleased to make a second, commonly called the Covenant of Grace: whereby he freely offereth unto sinners life and salvation by Jesus Christ, requiring of them faith in him, that they may be saved; and promising to give unto all those that are ordained unto life his Holy Spirit, to make them willing and able to believe."* (WCF VII:3)

   1. God cursed Adam, Eve, the serpent, and the earth after the Fall and yet promised the hope of a Messiah in Genesis 3:15.
   2. God made another covenant with man in the Covenant of Grace promising to crush the head of the serpent.
   3. God made a covenant with Abraham to choose a people for Himself as the beginnings of His kingdom.
   4. God made a covenant with Israel through Moses establishing His laws and the consequences of obedience and disobedience.

H. Man is justified by the works of Christ alone who satisfied the demands of the Law.
    1. The Covenant of Grace satisfies the demands of the Covenant of Works.
    2. The merit of Christ is the only effectual merit for justifying sinners.

I. The work of Christ is the substance of our justification and faith is the means of our justification.

J. The Roman Catholic position argued that man's righteousness must cooperate with the righteousness of God to demonstrate infused righteousness.

K. The Protestant Reformers argued for an imputed righteousness wherein man is declared fully righteous upon the regenerative act of God apart from any human works.
    - Man must receive the alien righteousness of Christ in order to be saved.

L. The righteousness of Christ is not from us, but it is for us.

M. A believer's righteousness is the imputed righteousness of Christ apart from any works of the believer.

STUDY QUESTIONS

1. ___________ argued that salvation is by grace alone, through faith alone, because of Christ alone.
    a. The Roman Catholic Church
    b. The Protestant Reformers
    c. The Pelagians
    d. The Semi-Pelagians

2. The basic structure of the relationship between God and His people is found in the ___________.
    a. Law
    b. covenants
    c. prophecies
    d. treasury of merit

3. Every covenant God offers to man is an act of ___________.
    a. grace
    b. compromise
    c. obligation
    d. duty

4. Adam and Eve were under a period of ___________ in the Garden wherein if they obeyed God they would have life and if they disobeyed God they would die.
    a. consummation
    b. sanctification
    c. regeneration
    d. probation

5. The Covenant of __________ satisfies the demands of the Covenant of __________.
   a. Works, Grace
   b. Grace, Hope
   c. Grace, Gospel
   d. Grace, Works

6. God made another covenant with man in the Covenant of __________ promising to crush the head of the serpent.
   a. Works
   b. Grace
   c. Hope
   d. Law

7. The Roman Catholic position argued that man's righteousness must cooperate with the righteousness of God to demonstrate __________ righteousness.
   a. imparted
   b. infused
   c. imputed
   d. impotent

8. The Protestant Reformers argued for an __________ righteousness wherein man is declared fully righteous upon the regenerative act of God apart from any human works.
   a. imparted
   b. infused
   c. imputed
   d. impotent

BIBLE STUDY

1. How does Christ place Himself at the center of the salvation process in John 5? Why is the intimate relationship Jesus describes between He and His Father essential for believers?

2. How is it that the dead can live according to John 5:25? In what sense are nonbelievers alive? Dead? In what sense are believers alive? Dead?

3. How does Jesus emphasize his exclusivity in John 5:31-47? How are you tempted to follow someone or something other than the person of Jesus Christ?

4. What is the relationship between Jesus and the Scriptures according to John 5:39-40? How are believers tempted to reverse this statement?

5. How were the Pharisees guilty of receiving others in their own name, but not Jesus who represented God (John 5:43)? How are believers tempted to emulate another person besides the person of Christ?

6. What promise does Jesus declare in John 8:12? What is the life that Jesus offers in this verse?

7. According to John 8:19 how can we know the character of God the Father and His attitude towards us? What is the Father's attitude towards you?

DISCUSSION QUESTIONS

1. Why does Jesus steer his disciples away from discouragement in John 14? Why can those who believe that Christ alone secures their salvation have joyful hearts? How is that joy temporal and eternal?

2. How does Jesus' claim in John 14:6 compare to the claims of other religious leaders? How do Jesus' words here give us guidance as we look for God's direction in our lives?

3. How does Roman Catholic theology substitute something different for the truth that salvation is through Christ alone? How are Protestants guilty of trying to add something to the finished work of Christ?

APPLICATION

1. Consider what it would currently mean in your life to follow Jesus rather than ideas about Jesus.

2. Meditate on the truth that Jesus' blood secures for you the approval and delight of the Father.

FOR FURTHER STUDY

Sproul, R.C. *Willing to Believe*
Sproul, R.C. *What is Reformed Theology?*
Robertson, O. Palmer *The Christ of the Covenants*
Ferguson, Sinclair *In Christ Alone*

6

Solus Christus

MESSAGE INTRODUCTION

There is no claim more offensive to a pluralistic culture than that Jesus provides the only access to God. Yet understanding the work of Christ alone as the only option for man's justification is fundamental to the Gospel itself. The life and death of Jesus were both essential to atone for the sins of men and bring them the righteousness a holy God requires. Justification is a double imputation wherein our sins are imputed to Jesus and His righteousness is imputed to us. In this lecture, Dr. Sproul discusses the truth that salvation is by Christ alone.

SCRIPTURE READING

Ephesians 1-2

LEARNING OBJECTIVES

1. To describe Christ's role as mediator of the New Covenant.
2. To distinguish between the active and passive obedience of Christ.
3. To distinguish between infused and imputed righteousness.

QUOTATION

"'There is but one God,' says St. Paul, 'and one mediator between God and man; namely, the man Jesus Christ, who gave himself a ransom for all.' Therefore, let no man think to draw near unto God or obtain grace of him, without this mediator, high priest, and advocate.

It follows that we cannot through our good works, honesty of life, virtues, deserts, sanctity, or through the works of the law, appease God's wrath, or obtain forgiveness of sins; and that all deserts of saints are quite rejected and condemned, so that through them no human creature can be justified before God. Moreover, we see how fierce God's anger is against sins, seeing that by none other sacrifice or offering could they be appeased and stilled, but by the precious blood of the Son of God."

—Martin Luther

LECTURE OUTLINE

A. The New Testament emphatically affirms that access to God is through Christ alone.

B. *"First of all, then, I urge that supplications, prayers, intercessions, and thanksgivings be made for all people, for kings and all who are in high positions, that we may lead a peaceful and quiet life, godly and dignified in every way. This is good, and it is pleasing in the sight of God our Savior, who desires all people to be saved and to come to the knowledge of the truth. For there is one God, and there is one mediator between God and men, the man Christ Jesus, who gave himself as a ransom for all, which is the testimony given at the proper time. For this I was appointed a preacher and an apostle (I am telling the truth, I am not lying), a teacher of the Gentiles in faith and truth."* (1 Tim. 2:1-7)

C. There is no claim more offensive to a pluralistic culture than the exclusivity of the person of Christ as a means of salvation.
   1. Jesus is the only mediator between God and man.
   2. The task of a mediator is to bring reconciliation between two estranged parties.
   3. Jesus is the mediator between the estranged parties of God and man.

D. The temporal mediators of Moses, the priests, and the prophets foreshadowed the greatest mediator in the person of Christ.
   - Only the Son of God can ultimately reconcile others to the Father.

E. The mediating work of Christ is referred to as the obedience of Christ.
   1. Jesus performs the work of mediation in His humanity.
   2. Jesus performs the role of the second Adam.

F. The obedience of Christ can be understood as the active obedience of Christ and the passive obedience of Christ.
   - The atonement for our sins that Christ accomplished on the cross is central to the Gospel.

G. The cross removes our demerits, but it offers us no merit or positive righteousness.
   1. The justification of believers requires more than Jesus' death.
   2. Jesus' death on the cross was the passive obedience of Christ.
   3. Jesus endured the punishment of the Father on the cross.

H. *"Surely he has borne our griefs and carried our sorrows; yet we esteemed him stricken; smitten by God, and afflicted. Yet it was the will of the Lord to crush him; he has put him to grief;"* (Isa. 53:4, 10a)
   1. Christ receives the curse of our sins on the cross at the hand of the Father.
   2. The Father insists that Jesus drink the cup of suffering despite His pleas to the contrary.
   3. The sacrifice of Jesus on the cross satisfies the demands of God's justice.

4. Jesus is the propitiation or satisfaction for God's justice on the cross.

I. Jesus not only died for our justification, but also lived for our justification.
   1. Jesus had to achieve perfect righteousness in His own life.
   2. Jesus was like us in every way except He was innocent of sin.
   3. Jesus is the only man to ever live a life of perfection.
   4. Death had no claim over Jesus because He lived a perfect life.
   5. The perfect life of Christ is referred to as the active obedience of Christ.

J. *"Then Jesus came from Galilee to the Jordan to John, to be baptized by him. John would have prevented him, saying, 'I need to be baptized by you, and do you come to me?' But Jesus answered him, 'Let it be so now, for thus it is fitting for us to fulfill all righteousness.' Then he consented."* (Matt. 3:13-15)
   1. John could not understand why the Messiah Himself would undergo a ritual pointing to the coming of the Messiah.
   2. Baptism indicated a cleansing from sin.
   3. It was necessary for Jesus to fulfill all righteousness, that is, obey every law God had established for His people.
   4. From his birth to his death Jesus actively obeyed every letter of the Law.

K. The basis of justification is the transfer or imputation of the righteousness of Christ to the believer.

L. Justification is a double imputation wherein our sins are imputed to Him and His righteousness is imputed to us.

M. The justification of believers is through Christ alone.

STUDY QUESTIONS

1. The New Testament emphatically affirms the exclusive access to God through ___________ alone.
   a. Christ
   b. faith
   c. grace
   d. Scripture

2. There is no claim more offensive to a pluralistic culture than the ___________ of the person of Christ as a means of salvation.
   a. universalism
   b. impossibility
   c. exclusivism
   d. inclusivism

3. The task of a ___________ is to bring reconciliation between two estranged parties.
   a. mediator
   b. judge
   c. propitiator
   d. expiator

4. The __________ of Christ can be divided into the active and passive.
    a. obedience
    b. forgiveness
    c. sanctification
    d. grace

5. The cross removes our demerits, but it offers us no merit or __________ righteousness.
    a. negative
    b. positive
    c. infused
    d. natural

6. Jesus' death on the cross was the __________ obedience of Christ.
    a. passive
    b. negative
    c. active
    d. natural

7. The perfect life of Christ is referred to as the __________ obedience of Christ.
    a. passive
    b. negative
    c. active
    d. natural

8. Justification involves a __________ imputation.
    a. single
    b. double
    c. triple
    d. quadruple

BIBLE STUDY

1. Why does Paul offer praise to God the Father in Ephesians 1:3? What are the spiritual blessings Paul is referring to here?

2. When did Christ begin to love and choose those whom He would redeem? What has always been the plan of God? How has He always intended on accomplishing this plan?

3. How did God secure the freedom of His children (1:7)? What is the inheritance of which Paul is speaking here?

4. Why does Paul label the redemptive plan of God a mystery in Eph. 1:9? What is the inheritance of which Paul is speaking here?

5 What does Paul indicate a believer receives upon conversion that shows he or she belongs to Christ (v. 13)? What is the significance of this gift?

6. What is the relationship between the grace Paul describes and the prayer he offers in Ephesians chapter one?

7. How does Paul describe a shift in kingdom citizenship for believers in Ephesians 2? What is the character of the citizens in each kingdom? Who is responsible for changing our citizenship?

8. How will the glorification of believers bring honor and praise to God for the rest of eternity according to Eph. 2:7? In what sense are believers trophies of God's grace?

DISCUSSION QUESTIONS

1. How does each member of the Trinity play a critical role in man's salvation according to Ephesians 1?

2. How does a change in kingdom citizenship affect each of the following areas of life?

a. relationships	c. marriage	e. work
b. worship	d. money	f. leisure

3. Why does Paul discuss the image of the Temple in Ephesians 2? What is the relationship between the work of Christ and the dwelling place of God?

APPLICATION

1. Meditate on the fact that God intended to adopt you into His family before your birth.

2. Reflect on the fact that you are a trophy of God's grace.

FOR FURTHER STUDY

Sproul, R.C. *Willing to Believe*
Sproul, R.C. *What is Reformed Theology?*
Ferguson, Sinclair *In Christ Alone*

7

Sola Scriptura

MESSAGE INTRODUCTION

The appearance of Martin Luther before the Diet of Worms in 1521 was one of the most dramatic moments in history. Luther took a bold stand against the Roman Catholic authorities by asserting the truths of the Gospel. The extraordinary part of Luther's argument was how he defended his writings. Luther argued that Scripture alone and not popes or councils had the exclusive power to bind the conscience of the Christian. In this lecture, Dr. Sproul discusses the absolute authority of Scripture alone.

SCRIPTURE READING

Psalm 19

LEARNING OBJECTIVES

1. To discuss the Reformed understanding of Scripture.
2. To explain Martin Luther's defense of the authority of Scripture.
3. To contrast the authority of Scripture with other authorities for the faith of a Christian.

QUOTATION

"No greater mischief can happen to a Christian people, than to have God's word taken from them, or falsified, so that they no longer have it pure and clear. God grant we and our descendants be not witnesses of such a calamity."

—Martin Luther

LECTURE OUTLINE

A. The question of authority in matters of faith sparked great debate during the Protestant Reformation.

B. *"The supreme judge by which all controversies of religion are to be determined, and all decrees of councils, opinions of ancient writers, doctrines of men, and private spirits, are to be examined, and in whose sentence we are to rest, can be no other but the Holy Spirit speaking in the Scripture."* (WCF I: X)

C. The Reformation began with Martin Luther posting the 95 Theses on the church door at Wittenberg seeking an academic debate regarding the sale of indulgences.
   1. Luther's Theses were spread throughout Germany by the printing press.
   2. Luther attacked the idea that the Pope had authority over a treasury of merit from which he could dispense the righteous merit of past saints.

D. Luther's theses were rejected and condemned by the Roman Catholic Church.
   - Fredrick the Elector of Saxony protected Luther from the Holy Roman Emperor and the church officials.

E. Luther was seeking to have a theological discussion regarding the theses he had posted and not cause division in the church.
   1. Luther secured an opportunity for theological discussion at Augsburg with the prestigious scholar Cardinal Cajetan.
   2. Cajetan quoted from a fourteenth century papal encyclical affirming a treasury of merit.
   3. Luther responded by pointing out that Cajetan had misquoted the encyclical.
   4. The debate revealed Luther had questions regarding the final authority of papal encyclicals.

F Luther debated at Leipzig in 1519 with John Eck who was considered one of the greatest scholars of the time.
   1. Eck showed how Luther was endorsing some of the articles of John Hus that were condemned at the Council of Constance.
   2. It was clear that Luther was guilty of questioning the decisions of church councils.

G. *"I assert that a council has sometimes erred and may sometimes err, nor has a council authority to establish new articles of faith. A council cannot make divine right out of that which is by nature is not divine right. Councils have contradicted each other. —* Martin Luther
   - Luther argued Scripture was the final authority for faith and practice and pope or councils cannot devise new doctrine.

H. The Diet of Worms was summoned in 1521 to resolve the growing theological dispute.
   1. Luther refused to recant his writings and teachings before the Emperor, cardinals, bishops, and legates of Rome.
   2. *"Unless I am convicted by Scripture and plain reason, I do not accept the authority of popes and councils, for they have contradicted each other. My*

conscience is captive to the Word of God. I cannot and I will not recant anything, for to go against conscience is neither right nor safe. God help me. Amen." —Martin Luther

3. Only God can bind the conscience absolutely.
4. Churches, people, and creeds are only binding on the Christian in as much they reflect the accuracy of Scripture.

STUDY QUESTIONS

1. The question of __________ sparked great debate during the Protestant Reformation.
   a. Christ's divinity
   b. authority
   c. God's existence
   d. evolution

2. The Reformation began with __________ posting the 95 Theses on church door at Wittenberg seeking an academic debate regarding the sale of indulgences.
   a. John Calvin
   b. John Knox
   c. Martin Luther
   d. John Huss

3. Luther attacked the idea that the Pope had authority over a __________ from which he could dispense the righteous merit of past saints.
   a. purgatory
   b. treasury of merit
   c. collection of relics
   d. church council

4. __________ protected Luther from the Holy Roman Emperor and the church officials.
   a. Cardinal Cajetan
   b. Frederick the Elector
   c. Philip Melanchthon
   d. Philip of Hesse

5. Luther secured an opportunity for theological discussion at Augsburg with the prestigious scholar __________.
   a. Cardinal Cajetan
   b. John Eck
   c. Joseph Spalatin
   d. Jerome Alexander

6. John Eck showed how Luther was endorsing some of the articles of __________ that were condemned at the Council of Constance.
   a. Peter Waldo
   b. Marcion
   c. John Huss
   d. Pelagius

7. Luther argued that __________ was the final authority for faith and practice.
   a. the Holy Spirit
   b. Scripture
   c. private revelation
   d. the pope

8. The Diet of Worms was summoned in __________ to resolve the growing theological dispute.
   a. 1519
   b. 1520
   c. 1521
   d. 1522

BIBLE STUDY

1. God reveals Himself through General Revelation, which is Creation and through Special Revelation which is His Word. How does the Psalmist celebrate God's revelation of Himself in nature in Ps. 19:1-6? How does the Psalmist celebrate God's revelation of Himself through His Word in Ps. 19:7-14?
2. In what sense does Creation speak without ever saying a Word? How do your favorite natural settings reveal the character of God to you? How do Creation and Scripture compare as sources of authority?
3. What do you believe the Psalmist was trying to highlight about God's character by discussing the sun in 19:4-6?
4. What kind of authority does the Psalmist attach to the Word of God in 19:7-8?
5. What impact do the commandments of God have on the heart according to 19:8? What is the attitude of the world towards God's Word and His commandments?
6. What is the value of the Word according to 19:12? What is the relationship between the conscience and the Word?
7. Why does the Psalmist conclude Psalm 19 by mentioning the words of his own mouth? What will the effect on our own lives be if we frequently listen to the Word of God?

DISCUSSION QUESTIONS

1. How does God speak through Scripture? How does He speak through Creation? What has He communicated to you through His General Revelation and Special Revelation?
2. Why are most people not believers if God truly reveals Himself through the natural world? What specifically does God reveal about Himself through Creation (cf. Rom. 1:20)
3. Why were the Reformers so insistent regarding Scripture as the final authority for faith and practice? What are the other lesser authorities for determining faith and practice?

APPLICATION

1. Ask the Lord to speak to you through His Word and creation.
2. Ask the Lord to use His Word to expose the deepest parts of your heart.

FOR FURTHER STUDY

Kistler, Don, ed. *Sola Scriptura*
Mathison, Keith *The Shape of Sola Scriptura*

8

Sola Scriptura

MESSAGE INTRODUCTION

The extent of Scripture's authority was an important question in the sixteenth century, and it still is today. The debate over scriptural authority led to questions surrounding how to interpret Scripture. The Roman Catholic Church asserted its exclusive right to interpret the Bible to the laity. The Protestant Reformers argued the Holy Spirit anoints each individual believer with the freedom to interpret Scripture responsibly and accurately. In this lecture, Dr. Sproul discusses the absolute authority of Scripture alone.

SCRIPTURE READING

Colossians 1

LEARNING OBJECTIVES

1. To discuss the relationship between the authority of Scripture and the authority of tradition.
2. To examine the decision of the Council of Trent regarding the relationship between Scripture and tradition.
3. To identify and define the Analogy of Faith.

QUOTATION

"Let us not lose the Bible, but with diligence, in fear and invocation of God, read and preach it. While that remains and flourishes, all prospers with the state; 'tis head and empress of all arts and faculties. Let but divinity fall, and I would not give a straw for the rest."

—Martin Luther

LECTURE OUTLINE

A. The extent of Scripture's authority was an important question in the sixteenth century and still is today.
   - The debate over Scriptural authority led to questions surrounding how to interpret Scripture.

B. *"The Holy, Ecumenical and General Council of Trent lawfully assembled in the Holy Ghost, the same three legates of the Apostolic See presiding, keeps this constantly in view, namely, that the purity of the Gospel may be preserved in the Church after the errors have been removed. This Gospel of old promised through the prophets in the Holy Scripture our Lord Jesus Christ the Son of God promulgated first with His own mouth and then commanded it to be preached by His apostles to every creature as the source at once of all saving truth and rules of conduct. It also clearly perceives that these truths and rules are contained in the written books and in the unwritten traditions which received by the apostles from the mouth of Christ Himself or from the apostles themselves the Holy Ghost dictating have come down to us transmitted as it were from hand to hand."*

   —The Fourth Session, The Council of Trent (1546)

   1. Great debate has surrounded this statement from the Council of Trent regarding the relationship between church traditions and Scripture.
   2. Does Scripture have greater authority or the same authority as the traditions of the Church?
   3. Earlier drafts of the Council of Trent stated the truths of the Gospel are found partly in Scripture and partly in tradition.
   4. There was debate within the Council itself regarding the final wording.

C. The Roman Catholic Church has emphasized the equal authority of Scripture and tradition since the Council of Trent.

D. Protestants emphasized the Spirit led power of individuals to privately interpret Scripture.

E. *"Furthermore to check unbridled spirits, it (the Council) decrees that no one relying on his own judgment shall in matters of faith and morals pertaining to the edification of Christian doctrine, distorting the Holy Scriptures in accordance with His own conceptions presume to interpret them contrary to that sense which Holy Mother Church to whom it belongs to judge the true sense in interpretation has held or holds or even contrary to the unanimous teaching of the Fathers even though such interpretations should never at any time be published. And those who act contrary to this should be known by the ordinaries and punished in accordance with the penalties prescribed by the law."*

F. The Protestant emphasis on the private interpretation of Scripture never sought to justify distorting Scripture's according to one's will.
   1. The right of interpretation comes with the responsibility of accuracy.

2. Many use the freedom to privately interpret Scripture as a justification for subjectivism today.
3. Scriptural texts contain one meaning yet many applications.

G. The Roman Catholic Church claims the exclusive right to interpret the meaning of Scriptural texts.
1. The Church argues that Scripture needs to be interpreted according to the tradition.
2. The Church also claims that Scripture received its authority in the first place from the Church itself.

H. The Reformers spoke of the Analogy of Faith regarding the authority of Scripture.
1. Sacred Scripture is interpreted by Scripture itself.
2. The Analogy of Faith assumes the unity and coherency of Sacred Scripture.

I. Scripture does not contradict itself and both the church and individuals should look to the Holy Spirit or author of Scripture to interpret the text itself.

STUDY QUESTIONS

1. The extent of Scripture's __________ was an important question in the sixteenth century and still is today.
   a. validity
   b. authority
   c. accuracy
   d. authenticity

2. Great debate has surrounded a statement from the Council of __________ regarding the relationship between church traditions and Scripture.
   a. Trent
   b. Constance
   c. Basle
   d. Chalcedon

3. The Roman Catholic Church has emphasized the equal authority of __________ and __________ since the Council of Trent.
   a. tradition, popes
   b. bishops, popes
   c. Scripture, tradition
   d. Scripture, popes

4. The __________ emphasized the Spirit-led power of individuals to privately interpret Scripture.
   a. Roman Catholics
   b. Protestants
   c. Gnostics
   d. Nestorians

5. Many use the freedom to privately interpret Scripture as a justification of __________ today.
   a. authoritarianism
   b. subjectivism
   c. exclusivism
   d. dogmatism

6. Scriptural texts contain one __________ yet many applications.
   a. translation
   b. meaning
   c. understanding
   d. illustration

7. The Reformers spoke of the Analogy of Faith regarding the authority of __________.
   a. the papacy
   b. Scripture
   c. councils
   d. pastors

8. The Analogy of Faith assumes the __________ and __________ of Sacred Scripture.
   a. translation, meaning
   b. meaning, application
   c. irrelevance, importance
   d. unity, coherency

BIBLE STUDY

1. How does Deuteronomy 6 serve as an important introductory speech to the rest of the book? Why does Moses plead passionately with the people in this chapter?

2. Why does Moses encourage the Israelites to obey the Law God has handed down in His Word? What does He predict will be the result of Israelites obedience?

3. Why would the confession of faith in Deut. 6:4-5 be so unique for the Israelites in the Ancient Near East? In what sense is the call to love, obey, and fear the Lord unique?

4. How does Moses encourage the Israelites to teach the Word in Deut. 6:6-9? How can believers today practically integrate the Word of God into their lives?

5. How will the Israelites be tempted when they enter the Promised Land according to Deut. 6:10-13? Why are the words "remember" and "forget" important to every believer?

6. What blessings does Moses promise the Israelites if they obey the Word of the Lord? Do these promised blessings apply to believers today? How or how not?

7. How are the Israelite parents to respond when their children ask them the meaning of God's Law? How would you respond if you were asked what is the significance of God's Word?

DISCUSSION QUESTIONS

1. What does Deut. 6 teach you about the source of authority in matters of faith and practice? What role does tradition play in this passage?

2. What kind of priority does Moses place on reading, knowing, and obeying the Word of God? How did the Reformers champion this cause as well?

3. How is the Word of God being rejected or trivialized today? What are other sources of truth that help us understand the absolute authority of the Word of God?

APPLICATION

1. Reflect on the authority the Word of God has over your life.

2. Ask the Lord to show you how to integrate the influence of your experience and other people with the absolute authority of Scripture.

FOR FURTHER STUDY

Kistler, Don, ed. *Sola Scriptura*
Mathison, Keith *The Shape of Sola Scriptura*

9

Soli Deo Gloria

MESSAGE INTRODUCTION

Among the great themes of the Protestant Reformation, there was no greater emphasis than the glory of God. The Reformers sought to elevate the eternal God of glory in everything they wrote and taught. The glory of God is not taken lightly in Scripture. In fact, the very word carries with it heavy connotations. Theology that does not exalt the glory of God as the ultimate reality in the universe is not theology but heresy. In this lecture, Dr. Sproul discusses the Reformer's emphasis on God's glory alone.

SCRIPTURE READING

1 Corinthians 15

LEARNING OBJECTIVES

1. To explain the Reformer's emphasis on the glory of God alone.
2. To trace the Old Testament understanding of the glory of God.
3. To link the glory of God with the person of Jesus.

QUOTATION

"Who is this King of glory? The Lord of hosts, he is the king of glory."

—Psalm 24:10

LECTURE OUTLINE

A. Soli Deo Gloria was the overarching theme of the Reformation as it means "To God alone is the glory."

B. The first question of the Westminster Shorter Catechism is "what is the chief end of man?"
   1. The answer to the question is "Man's chief end is to glorify God and enjoy Him forever."
   2. Paul told the Corinthians that whether they eat or drink they should do all to glorify God.
C. The English word "glory" comes from the Latin word gloria, the Greek word doxa, and the Hebrew word kabod.
   - The Hebrew word kabod means "weightiness" or "heaviness".
D. The glory of God refers to His importance, dignity, and significance.
   1. God is a not a creature, but rather the Creator.
   2. God is to be treated with ultimate weight and importance.
E. The Doxology and the Gloria Patri are two songs the church sings to ascribe glory to God alone.
F. God declares in Scripture that He will share His glory with no man.
G. *"For not all flesh is the same, but there is one kind for humans, another for animals, another for birds, and another for fish. There are heavenly bodies and earthly bodies, but the glory of the heavenly is of one kind, and the glory of the earthly is of another. There is one glory of the sun, and another glory of the moon, and another glory of the stars; for star differs from star in glory."* (1 Cor. 15: 39-41)
   1. Man does not share God's glory, but reflects it to the rest of creation.
   2. Man holds dignity because God ascribes dignity to His image bearers.
   3. One cannot ascribe dignity to man without acknowledging the glory of God.
   4. Only the God of eternal glory holds inherent and intrinsic glory.
H. Moses asked God to show him His glory face to face.
   1. God refuses because no man can see the face of God and live.
   2. God shows Moses his back and Moses' face is radiant.
   3. The radiance of Moses' face was a reflection of God's glory.
I. The clothes and appearance of Christ were transfigured on the Mount of Olives before the eyes of Peter, James, and John.
   1. The disciples fell on their faces in fear and trembling.
   2. The light that emanated from the presence of Christ on the Mount was not a reflected glory, but inherent to His person as the Son of God.
   3. The glory of God filled the sky on the night of Christ's birth.
   4. The writer of Hebrews describes Jesus as the express image of God's person and the brightness of His glory.
   5. John describes Jesus as the Word and His glory as of the Son from the Father.
J. All the glory for man's salvation belongs to God alone, that is, Soli Deo Gloria.
   - God initiates and accomplishes salvation from beginning to end.
K. Worship is to be directed towards God's glory alone.

STUDY QUESTIONS

1. __________ was the overarching theme of the Reformation.
   a. Soli Deo Gloria
   b. "Love your neighbor"
   c. "Live free or die"
   d. "Trust and obey"

2. The __________ question of the Westminster Shorter Catechism is "what is the chief end of man?"
   a. first
   b. second
   c. third
   d. fourth

3. Paul told the __________that whether they eat or drink they should do all to glorify God.
   a. Corinthians
   b. Ephesians
   c. Colossians
   d. Philippians

4. The English word __________ comes from the Latin word gloria, the Greek word doxa, and the Hebrew word kabod.
   a. hope
   b. faith
   c. love
   d. glory

5. The Hebrew word __________ means "weightiness" or "heaviness".
   a. nissi
   b. ish
   c. nascar
   d. kabod

6. The __________ and the Gloria Patri are two songs the church sings to ascribe glory to God alone.
   a. Ava Maria
   b. Benedictus
   c. Magnificat
   d. Doxology

7. __________ asked God to show him His glory face to face.
   a. Gideon
   b. Jacob
   c. Elisha
   d. Moses

8. The writer of Hebrews describes __________ as the express image of God's person and the brightness of His glory.
   a. creation
   b. the heavens
   c. Jesus
   d. the resurrection

BIBLE STUDY

1. What is the constant attitude of the Corinthians towards receiving the Gospel? Why does the message of the true Gospel fail to grow dull for believers? What is happening when the message of the Gospel does seem to grow dull?

2. What were some of the Corinthians claiming regarding the resurrection from the dead (v. 12-19)? Why does Paul insist upon the truth of this doctrine?

3. How does God place His glory as preeminent in the order of resurrection (v. 20-25)? How is man's resurrection a reflection of God's glory?

4. How is there a growing crescendo towards God's glory in 1 Cor. 15:21-28? How is Christ and His kingdom currently on the march against His enemies?

5. What will be the gift Christ delivers to the Father upon complete victory? How is the glory of the Father the mission of Christ?

6. Why does Paul have the confidence to risk death daily according to 1 Corinthians 15:30-32? Why should believers be able to exhibit the most courage of all men and women?

7. How will man reflect the glory of God in their bodies after the resurrection? How will this reflection be the same or different as it is presently?

DISCUSSION QUESTIONS

1. Why is the glorious resurrection of Christ a distinctive part of orthodox Christianity? Why is it fundamental to any true confession of faith?

2. How do believers currently wage war against Christ's enemies to bring in the kingdom of glory?

3. Give examples from your own life as to how you personally reflect the glory of God.

APPLICATION

1. Consider how you can remind others that they bear the image of God.

2. Ask the Lord to show you how you can fight against His enemies and bring in His glorious kingdom.

FOR FURTHER STUDY

Sproul, R.C. *What is Reformed Theology?*
Sproul, R.C. Jr. *After Darkness Light*

10

Soli Deo Gloria

MESSAGE INTRODUCTION

The Protestant Reformers emphasized giving God complete glory in the salvation of man and the worship of God. Yet they realized that the fundamental sin of humanity is idol worship and that by nature we are idol factories. The essence of idolatry is worshiping a substitute in the place of God. Humans have invented numerous ways of refusing to ascribe to God the glory due His name. God is seeking people to worship Him in Spirit and in truth. In this lecture, Dr. Sproul discusses soli Deo gloria.

SCRIPTURE READING

Revelation 19-22

LEARNING OBJECTIVES

1. To highlight the Reformer's emphasis on ascribing glory to God alone.
2. To define and explain the nature of idolatry.
3. To emphasize the role of God's glory in true worship.

QUOTATION

"So, whether you eat or drink, or whatever you do, do all to the glory of God."

—1 Cor. 10:31

LECTURE OUTLINE

A. The Reformers emphasized giving God complete glory in the salvation of man and the worship of God.
   1. Martin Luther's emphasis was on giving God complete glory in the salvation of man.

2. John Calvin's emphasis was on giving God complete glory in worship.
3. Bach was motivated to write his music for the purpose of God's glory.

B. Iconography plays a strong role in historic Roman Catholic worship.
1. The papacy discouraged worship of the statues, but encouraged veneration and service to the icons.
2. The Virgin Mary was also to be revered and serviced, but not worshipped.

C. Calvin said the fundamental sin of humanity is idol worship and that by nature we are idol factories.

D. *"For the wrath of God is revealed from heaven against all ungodliness and unrighteousness of men, who by their unrighteousness suppress the truth. For what can be known about God is plain to them, because God has shown it to them. For his invisible attributes, namely, his eternal power and divine nature, have been clearly perceived, ever since the creation of the world, in the things that have been made. So they are without excuse. For although they knew God, they did not honor him as God or give thanks to him, but they became futile in their thinking, and their foolish hearts were darkened. Claiming to be wise, they became fools, and exchanged the glory of the immortal God for images resembling mortal man and birds and animals and reptiles."* (Rom. 1:18-23)
1. All of humanity is under God's judgment not because they reject Jesus of whom they have never heard, but rather the Father who testifies of Himself in creation.
2. Nobody in all of creation has an excuse for rejecting God.
3. The basic element in humanity's corruption is a refusal to properly glorify God.

E. The essence of idolatry is worshipping a substitute in the place of God.
- Sin is always an exchange of truth for a lie.

F. Stripping God of one or more of His attributes is also a form of idolatry.
1. We worship the idol of our own thoughts if we ignore the love, justice, mercy, wrath, sovereignty, or freedom of God Almighty.
2. The idea that all faiths or all gods worshipped are equally valuable is a lie and a form of idolatry.
3. Man made religion is just as much idolatry as paganism itself.

G. God is seeking people to worship Him in Spirit and in truth.

H. The Cambridge Declaration issued a statement emphasizing the sole glory of God as the focus of worship.

I. The point of our salvation must be the glory of God.

STUDY QUESTIONS

1. The __________ emphasized giving God complete glory in the salvation of man and the worship of God.
   a. papacy
   b. Nestorians
   c. Reformers
   d. Gnostics

2. Iconography plays a strong role in historic __________ worship.
   a. Reformed
   b. Baptist
   c. Roman Catholic
   d. Puritan

3. The __________ papacy discouraged worship of the statues, but encouraged veneration and service to the icons.
   a. Reformed
   b. Baptist
   c. Roman Catholic
   d. Puritan

4. __________ said the fundamental sin of humanity is idol worship and that by nature we are idol factories.
   a. Martin Luther
   b. John Calvin
   c. Pope Leo X
   d. John Wesley

5. All of humanity is under God's judgment not because they reject Jesus of whom they have never heard, but rather the Father who testifies of Himself in __________.
   a. the Bible
   b. church
   c. the sacraments
   d. creation

6. The essence of __________ is worshipping a substitute in the place of God.
   a. Reformed worship
   b. idolatry
   c. Roman Catholic worship
   d. Lutheran worship

7. Stripping God of one or more of His attributes is also a form of __________.
   a. Reformed worship
   b. idolatry
   c. Roman Catholic worship
   d. Lutheran worship

8. The idea that all faiths or all gods worshipped are equally valuable is a lie and a form of ________.
    a. orthodoxy
    b. authoritarianism
    c. orthopraxy
    d. idolatry

BIBLE STUDY

1. How does Revelation 19:1 provide a fitting introduction and summary of the final chapters of the book of Revelation? Why are the saints so ecstatic in Rev. 19:1-10?

2. How does Jesus gain glory for Himself over His enemies in Rev. 19:11-21? How are the saints blessed to participate?

3. How does Satan the ancient serpent try to steal the glory of God? What are the deceptions he brings against you?

4. Describe the scene of the great white throne judgment from Rev. 20:11-15. How is God glorified in the judgment of the wicked?

5. What are the metaphors for the New Jerusalem John uses to convey God's glory in Rev. 21? How will God restore the glory of the earth by making all things new?

6. What role will God's glory play in the New Jerusalem according to Rev. 22:3-5?

DISCUSSION QUESTIONS

1. How will believers experience the glory of God in the restored kingdom? How will believers participate in His majesty?

2. How do Satan and his followers contribute to God's glory at the end of the age? Does sin contribute or not contribute to the glory of God?

APPLICATION

1. Reflect on the contrast between what your life is like now and what it will be like in the New Jerusalem.

2. Reflect on how God has turned the inglorious into something glorious in your life.

FOR FURTHER STUDY

Sproul, R.C. *Essential Truths of the Christian Faith*
Sproul, R.C. Jr. *After Darkness Light*